It was some of the things that I've experienced, it was some of the things that I've encountered, and It was some of the things that I've endured that made me frustrated, it was all of those things that leads me to take action, it was all of those things that I've conveyed through Rhythm And Poetry, it's my thoughts, and it's my words.

Down & Dirty Publishing

©2016 By Dirty Dollars

ISBN 978-0-9986098-1-7

Library of Congress Control Number 2017901626

"It is hard to fail, but it is worse never to have tried to succeed."

Theodore Roosevelt

"Failure is simply the opportunity to begin again, this time more intelligently."

Henry Ford

"Success is going from failure to failure with no loss of enthusiasm."

Winston Churchill

I'm Frustrated Thoughts Becoming Words

Frustrated: to disappoint; to prevent from attaining a goal or fulfilling a desire, to cause feelings of discouragement or bafflement.

I became frustrated at the age of five years old. I was overwhelmed with feelings of discouragement as I laid in solitude, I stretched my legs in the midst of silence in my small room. It was painted pale white, it was a small box with a dark wooden stained door that always stayed shut. My bedroom had a sand blasted ceiling that I use to stare at, I use to gaze at it during painful moments of reflection. I laid there upon my back in an oak wooden, red and white decorated, twin size bed on that quiet afternoon. My frowned eyes were filled with tears that I struggled to release, I tried hard to hold them back, but they rolled onto my pillow when I looked at the matching red and white

dresser that completed my bedroom set. It belonged to my Mother, she use to sleep in that same bed, and she used that same dresser as a young adult before she left the nest.

I was in pain as I visualized my mother. My momma had received a Life Sentence for Murder in the 1st Degree back in

1983. It was hard for me to imagine what Life in prison meant at the age of five years old. I had the slightest idea of what my life would become at the age of five. I was frustrated because I wanted her care, and I needed her love. I was upset because I wanted her affection, and I needed her attention. My Mother was my partner in crime, and I was her advocate. She allowed me to be myself as a child, and she allowed me to express myself as a child. She shaped my character, she carefully molded me into a Little Man.

I had taken on special duties that she assigned to me, such as; babysitting my infant baby brother while she took a nap. I use to hold his baby bottle for him while he ate, and I would get it for him every time he playfully tossed it to the ground.

 My little brother was only one year old when our Mother got sent to prison. When our momma got locked up, it was a sudden change for the both of us. He was sent to stay with his daddy's momma, while I stayed at our other Grandma's house. It was those relevant changes that confused me as a child, I felt bafflement in those sudden changes, and it showed in my demeanor. I laid there anticipating her return, I laid there speculating her departure with my tiny fist balled up in preparation to strike something, or someone.

"Bang!" I angrily punched my head board, and I felt the sting shoot through my knuckles. This was just the beginning of my feelings of discouragement, this was just the start of my feelings of confusion.

I was frustrated because I was being punished by my grandmother who was my guardian at that particular time in my life.

"Boy I tell ya...you're a pain in the butt," She said. "Get out of my sight!" She shouted.

She directed me towards my bedroom after she had disciplined me for hitting another child at school.

I was lashing out, I was acting up, and I was frustrated. I released an angry sigh as I browsed my dimly lit room.

The sun began to escape into another part of the region as night fell upon us. I could hear the sounds of the cars from a short distance. They quickly came; and they quickly went up and down Topping Street, they seemed to be hydroplaning down the steep wet heel on that rainy evening.

I became curious to see what the automobiles looked like as I laid there. I eased off of my bed, and I peeked through the mini blinds that were neatly positioned behind a pair of red and white colored curtains. It was a ray of light that beamed inside of my room, it shined brightly as I peeked. I took a brief glimpse at the street light that was on the corner of 21st St., it illuminated a tall wooden sign that advertised Park Tower Town Homes. My eyes shifted. Then I briefly took notice of the other street light that stood at the end of our block.

The modern low income housing projects that were located on 23rd & Topping, they extended all the way to 17th & Topping. There were approximately 304 units that aligned the hills of numerous blocks on the east side of Kansas City, Missouri. We stayed at 2017 Topping on a square block that sat on top of a steep heel. It was two other apartment buildings on our block that were properly constructed in front of forest green bushes, one of the apartment buildings was to the east of our building, and the other apartment building was facing south of our apartment.

There were several automobiles that were parked in front of each apartment. The old school whips appeared to be shaped like metal battleships as I observed them in various shapes and in different colors.

I noticed tiny pieces of asphalt blowing in the midst of the night's breeze. There were brown, orange, and tainted green leaves that had fallen from the tree in front of our apartment. They silently danced in our front yard, they tumbled over one another, and they tumbled amongst one another as the wind blew. The wind whistled loudly as it abruptly seeped through the cracks of the metal window frame, and it chilled my tiny chest.

There were moist circles of steam on the window that had formed from the heat that escaped from my nostrils. I noticed the accumulation of dust that aligned at the bottom of my bedroom window seal when I looked down, I saw small cod webs in the corners of it when I looked up. My eyes shifted from corner to corner for a moment.

I silently gazed out of my bedroom window, and I silently began to reason with myself. It was that particular spot where I chilled, it was that exact spot where I meditated whenever I was on punishment.

I was an ornery little dude, I was a knucklehead, I was extra mannish, I was always on punishment, and I had plenty of time to analyze my demeanor.

"That's stupid," I said with a frown on my face after I thought of some of her strict rules. I became accustom to the new rules at my Grandma's house on that evening. I had to acknowledge them because they absorbed in my mind during angry moments of reflection. Although many of her rules seemed absurd, I finally realized that I must follow them accordingly to alleviate my constant days of punishment.

I use to get frustrated every time my Grandmother constantly insisted that I said; "Yes or no," instead of me shaking my head, yes or no. It would nag me every time she constantly insisted that I said, "Yes" instead of me saying, "Yeah."

"Dang..." I once said underneath my breath.

"Boy what!" she shouted. "Hold on, you aren't running nothing!"She hollered.

It would irritate me every time she corrected my bad manners, it would aggravate me every time she addressed my negative attitude towards her discipline. She constantly insisted that I control my aggression, and she constantly insisted that I handle my fury.

My Grandma was one of the key people that helped build my character as a child, she was one of the individuals who molded me into a respectful young man. She always showed me how to overcome adversity, she always instilled good morals and positive values in me, and she always showed me right from wrong. I love, I honor, and I respect my Grandmother, "Thank God for Grandma." She raised me the same way that she raised my five Uncles, but slightly different from how she raised my Aunt, and my Mother. She raised us to become responsible men, and she raised them to become reliable women. She nurtured me, she clothed me, and she fed me. She did all of those things, and she did all of them while keeping a roof over our heads. I was raised in a warm and cozy, low-class household. My Grandmother was never late paying her rent, and she was never late paying her bills because she went to work every day.

I learned how to move under the radar of my Grandma. I received hands on training from my youngest Uncle. He already had 15 years of prior experience with breaking the barriers of my Grandma's discipline, and he was qualified at properly negotiating with her. My youngest uncle is only ten years older than me, back then; he was fifth-teen years old when I was only five.

He use to pick me up from Head Start after he got out of school because he had to watch me while Grandma was at work. I remember how he would school me on how to play it, and I can recall how he briefly tried to teach me how to elude the discipline of my Grandma.

"Momma is something else when she gets mad," He said. "All you have to do is, do whatever she asks you to do, and you won't be on punishment all the time."

"You're a bad little rascal, boy. You have to start listening, Little Man," He said.

We paused for a second on the corner of 21s t & Terr. as an older model Ford LTD bent the corner. I could see a reflection of the noon sun in its clean windshield as it eased passed us. I blinked my eyes before I lowered my head then I slowly grabbed his hand so he could guide me across the street. My fat shoe laces where dangling from the sides of my shoes as I slowly walked. I saw a widening hole at the toe of my worn out Pro-wing tennis shoes as I moved along. I observed the freshly paved street on 21s t and Terr. for a moment after we stopped.

"Boy, tie your shoes," He said. I looked him in the eyes, and I mugged him for a moment. I noticed the wrinkles across his forehead; they were twisting his frowned face. It was a slight snare around his lips. I looked him up and down, as if to say, "Are you serious?"

"Boy, what are you waiting on?" He asked me.

I harbored a lot of animosity in me as a child, and it showed in my actions at that moment, frustration surfaced in the both of us. I instantly got tense from the sudden change in his temperament. I felt confused when he directed me to tie up my shoes, and I felt embarrassed because I did not know how to. A few seconds had passed while we stared at one another like two pit bulls prepared to lock on one another.

"You think your bad," he said after he jumped at me right before he laced me up.

The monotonous months progressed into the conclusion of a year, it progressed sunrise after sunrise, and it progressed moon after moon. "Boy you're growing like a weed, Little Man!" My Step Daddy said. He told me that every time that he dropped my little brother off over to Grandma's house.

I was growing into a bothersome little boy, and I started to evolve into a misfit, I was a ticking time bomb that was waiting to explode. I formed a passive-aggressive personality, I was a mannish little dude who annihilates things, I became violent, and I became belligerent, I became rough, and I became rugged.

In the midst of my neighborhood my behavior was bizarre. I stayed into trouble, and I stayed into fights.

It was a muggy summer evening, I could hear the chatter of the crickets from afar, there were a couple of bumble bees buzzing around the building, the shadow of the two story townhomes blocked the scorching summer sun. We sat in the shade on my porch, and we played on hot summer days. There was a delightful look on everyone's face, everyone laughed loudly, we were cracking up as we drove one another.

"Yo momma's so broke that she can't pay attention!"

"Ah! Ha! Ha! Ha!" Everyone chuckled, everyone except for me.

"Punk!" "Don't you be talkin bout my momma!" I yelled. The momma jokes use to be fighting words to me, I use to take them personal. I jumped at him, and I tried to grab him.

"Ha! Ha! Ha! Ha!" He chuckled as he clumsily slipped my grasp, he giggled as he swiftly ran through the grass. "You better run!" I shouted. "I'm going to jack him up," I mumbled to myself. I was furious because I couldn't catch him.

Way back in the days when we were younger, we raced our Big Wheels down the heels, and we played football in the summer. We either went to their house; or we went to my house

for something to eat, and then we'll rush to the streets for a game of hide and go seek. We reaped havoc in the square radius of those two blocks, we joust, and we fought. We all grew up rough in the ghetto. In the ghetto; when we played Cops & Robbers, it was always more kids that wanted to be Robbers instead of being Cops.

In the ghetto there were numerous examples of violence, it was numerous examples of ridicule, and it was more than enough sarcasm in the hood to contaminate the youth. It was the majority of us in the ghetto; at least nearly every young person in the hood who implemented those same characteristics. During the early eighties, we all implemented a Ghetto Attitude to Maintain in any Environment, everybody mimic the same behavior. It was a certain way that we walked in the hood, and it was a certain way that we talked in the hood.

"Those are fresh, or those are sporty." That's how the youth complimented one another's swag or style while we pimped walked down the street. In the eighties; every youth in our hood use to beat box, every kid wore Adidas or Fila, and it was during those years that I was introduced to Hip-Hop.

In the ghetto; Hip-Hop music instantly dominated our community, it rapidly absorbed into our culture because it was popular amongst the youth.

I remember the days of listening to My Uncle and his partners beatbox and rhyme at the park in front of the office on 21st St. I use to watch them, and I use to listen to them while they did their thing.

"You kick tha beat, and I'll bust a rhyme." Those were the days of the Fat Boyz and Curtis Blow.

It was around that time that I went to Milton Moore Elementary School on 31st & Spruce. It was my second grade year that I moved with my other Uncle, I moved in with him in the middle of the school year. He had just received a multi- million dollar settlement after he had an accident at work, and he lost both of his legs. I moved from 2017 Topping in Park Tower Town Homes, and I moved to 2510 Grand in The San Francisco Towers with my Uncle, we stayed two doors down from George Brett in suite #804. I slept in a Queen Size bed in between satin sheets. I rode to school, and I rode from school every day in a triple black Lincoln Limo.

I remember when my Uncle had gave me twenty one dollar bills before school one day. We sat in silence for a moment. We were parked on the side of the grade school. I looked out of the tinted window of the Limo while I waited for his chauffeur to come and open up my door for me. I was filled with joy as we sat there. I looked at him with a Kool-Aid grin on my face when the driver reached for the door handle. I was trying to count how many chocolate milks I could buy at lunch while I admired him. He sat there in an Adidas sweat suit, and he wore matching Adidas tennis shoes. He clutched a wooden grain Cain; he tightly gripped its golden handle. "I'll see you later Unc," I said.

But, before I could ease out of the Limo with the money that he gave me, he had looked at me, and he had said; "Little Man, I want you to give all of your friend's one dollar, then I want you to give the rest of the bread to the rest of the kids in your class, and I want you to keep one dollar for your lunch."
"That ought to buy you a couple of chocolate milks, shouldn't it?" He asked.
"Yeah..." I slowly answered.
"Alright then," He said.
"O.K. then," I said before I stepped out of the limousine.
"Damn..."I whispered to myself after I closed the door. The following weekend after that, he gave me forty dollars, it was two crispy twenty dollar bills.
"Go down stairs and get yourself something nice." He stuttered before he coughed with a joint hanging out of his mouth.
I caught the elevator down to the third floor, and I walked through the quiet hallway until I reached the door that lead to another corridor that connected The San Francisco Towers to the Crown Center Shopping Mall, I noticed the brick red floor tile after I closed the door, I walked through the corridor,

and I stepped into Crown Center. I went, and I bought the Fat Boyz record, and I got the Kurtis Blow album after I went to the movies.

I learned a lot from my Uncle, he was a good guardian. He taught me how to be dependable, and he taught me how to be reliable. My OG uncle was cooler than a fan, he showed me how to multiply on my hands one day when he was helping me with my homework.

It was the beginning of my third grade year in elementary school, it was around the end of the first semester. I was in class, I sat there examining my #2 pencil, I tested its durability for a moment before I looked at the Teacher. "O.K. class it's time for recess," She said. "Yea!" We shouted. The entire class was excited.

We happily skipped through the hall, and we happily followed each other out to the playground. My homeboy and me, we were the last two kids out of the building. I followed behind him as he hopped down the stairs. He stopped, and he stood behind a tree, and he took a piss. I followed behind him. I stopped, and I stood on the other side of the tree, and I took a piss.

"What are you two doing?" The teacher shouted as she rushed towards us. "You two head to the principal's office," She said. It was a matter of minutes before we were both standing in the principal's office.

"You stand on that corner." She directed my homeboy to the corner.

"And you! I want you to stand on that corner." She directed me to the opposite corner.

"I want the both of you to stand there until the end of recess," She said.

About ten minutes had passed while I stared at the marvel floor of the principal's office. I heard a woman's voice behind me. I looked back. "Damn..."I whispered to myself. I quickly turned back around.

"Little Man! Come here!" My auntie shouted. She had showed up to surprise me for lunch.

She angrily grabbed me by the hand; she angrily lead me up to the conference room, and she angrily whipped by butt.

I got the business from my OG Uncle after I got home from school. He mugged me when he looked me in my eyes before he socked me in my chest.

"You have to stop being mannish," He said after he chastised me.

I watched him as he waddled off on the nubs of his legs. It was a matter of minutes before he returned with my Big Chief writing tablet, and my number two pencil in his hand. It was quiet while I watched him quickly scribble on the tablet, he wrote for at least five minutes before he handed it to me.

"Here...Write those sentences."

"One hundred of them," He said.

"Damn," I mumbled to myself after I saw the long three paragraphs that he wrote out for me. The first five words at the beginning of the first paragraph,I can not forget because they instantly grabbed me, they stated; "I will not be mannish..."

All of a sudden tragedy struck in our household, it was an abrupt turn of events in a matter of weeks. My "OG" Uncle had been accused of Murder, he was charge with the murder of some guy. I stayed with him until the end of my third grade year.

I moved in with my Grand Daddy R.I.P, he stayed on 69t h and Bellefontaine, he owned the house at 6932 Bellefontaine.

My GrandDaddy was an old school slick cat, he was an old school gangster that settled in to the SouthEast part of Kansas City, Missouri after he finished serving a life sentence behind the walls.

I remember the first day that I settled in at his house. It was a King Size bed in the middle of the dining room floor; it sat in front of a 50" T.V. that had an old school cable box connected to it, it was a double barrel shotgun propped up against the corner next to a glass dining room table that was pushed back against the wall, and it was a 38 revolver on top of it. I looked at my Grand Daddy while he talked to me.

"If you're going to do something wrong, you make sure that you do it all by yourself because you can't tell on yourself," He told me. It was a serious look on his face, he gestured as he talked to me.

"I can't believe that nigga did some stupid ass shit like that, he could've paid me! and I would've of did it!" He said.

He started laughing before he coughed, and I laughed along with him.

"Come on Little Man, jab!" He shouted. He had both of his hands raised with his palms facing me.

"Jab!" I swung wildly at his palms.

"Naw, naw, naw," He said. "Wait a minute, hold ya hands up," He said.

"Hold'em up!" He raised his voice, and he hyped me up. I quickly held up my hands, and I stood in a boxer's stance.

"Jab, jab, bang!" "Jab, jab, bang!" He said as he swiftly threw his hands.

My GrandDaddy prepared me for battle, and he shaped me for the same fight that every Black Man across America fights, it's a perilous dispute over respect.

"Respect those that respect you, I don't care if they're grown ups or not," He said one afternoon before I went outside.

"If they cuss at you, you better cuss they ass back out, and if they hit you, you better hit they ass back, and then you come and get me." He told me.

My Grandfather showed me a lot of things. He taught me how to be responsible. I use to shovel the snow, and I use to cut the grass, I had to wash the dishes, and I had to take out the trash. He taught me how to change a flat tire, and he showed me where the car battery was.

My Granddaddy didn't play, he didn't play that slick shit,

trying to be slick got me sent to the dog house often.

"Hit the dog house," He said on one cold evening.

I looked at him for a moment, and my heart dropped. He pointed, and he directed me towards the front door. He had a thick gray afro, his bushy eyebrows were frowned, and it was a tattoo of a heart with an arrow going through it on his muscular arm.

"Damn," I thought. I knew what time it was. I fell asleep before I washed the dishes, and I didn't vacuum the front room, I was trying to be slick and he knew it. My GrandDaddy didn't play when it came to me doing my chores. I stayed in the dog house.

I stood in silence in the dank basement, it was dark, and it was cold. I stood there for at least an hour and a half; it had got dark outside. I stood there motionless for what seemed like an endless moment before I heard our dog barking, and then I heard footsteps outside of the basement door.

"Come on out of there," He said. He looked me in the eyes when we reached the side of the house, and he said; "You better not forget to wash those dishes again, you get in the house."

My GrandDaddy was as cold as the winter, and he was even dirtier than the hundred dollar bills that he would fold and hold. He kept a roll of dough that could choke a mule. GrandDaddy's house wasn't nothing like Grandma's house, it wasn't a warm and cozy home, it was a cold and hard household.

My GrandDaddy was a hustler, he use to sale dope, our door stayed open in the midst of the winter breeze. I formed a hard core mentality in the presence of my Granddaddy. He shaped me into a hustler, and it wasn't long before he molded me into a baby gangster.

I spent my fourth, and my fifth grade year staying with my Grandfather. I attended Blenheim Elementary School on Gregory & Prospect. I walked to and I walked from school every day. I learned how to play thumps, I learned how to play pencil break, and I also learned how to rap.

About five or six years rapidly passed, and Momma had been locked up for over half of a decade. It was the summer of 1989, and it was talk amongst the grown-ups in the family of momma getting out early on a furlough if she maintained good behavior. I prayed for that day, but my prayers went unanswered.

My momma got into a fight, and the parole board set her parole hearing back for another two years. I felt numb without my Mother, I waddled in discouragement, but I hide the way that I felt. I became noncompliant, I became irrational, I was nonconformant, and I was unwilling to compromise with authority.

You know what they say, "God might not come when you call him, but he's always on time." I was Eleven years old when I moved back in with my Grandma.

It was September 4, 1989, that was the month, the day, and the year that I turned twelve years old, it was the day that I hit puberty, and it was also the same date that I started to attend West Port Middle School, it was my sixth grade year. I was in a different world, it was bigger, and it was faster. I was in the midst of teenagers, and I was on the verge of becoming a teen myself.

You were considered to be cool if you wore the latest fashion, and you were considered to be cool if you mimic the latest style. All of the boys wore flat top haircuts or jerry curls, and we wore British Knights, or Troop tennis shoes. All of the girls wore several big ear rings in their ears, they had their nose pierced, they wore their hair in full perms with bangs, and they wore biking shorts. Those were the days of NWA, ICE-T, Too Short, and Scarface. The movies of those days were Krush Groove, Colors, and New Jack City. Those films had a big influence on the majority of the teens that struggled to establish an identity.

The majority of the kids at my school wanted to either be Hip-Hop B-Boys, Dope Men, or Gang Bangers. I had chose the gang life, I had become a Blood, and it's Blood in, and Blood out. I started ditching class with the seventh, and the eighth grade boys, we use to run the halls. I glorified, and I idealize the gangster lifestyle of some of the gangster rappers that I use to listen to. I went from spitting nursery rhymes to writing my own gangster raps, I had recorded a song called "Playing the role of a gangster" with K Crim on a old school tape player back in 1991.

I gripped the wooden rail that aligned the two tone painted wall before I quickly paced down the marble stairs two steps at a time. I hopped onto the landing only a few short steps from the huge stained windows of the aging Middle School before I eased down the second flight of stairs that lead me down to the second floor. I tightly gripped my three-ring binder along with the two Social Studies books that I carried when I reached the bottom of the stairs. It was a row of lockers that aligned the wall, they were about ten to fifth-teen feet in front of me. I quickly weaved in and out of a crowd of students who were also late getting to their second hour class. I finally reached my locker at the same time that the bell rung. I noticed two young men quickly headed in my direction.

I fondled with my books inside of my locker for a moment before I looked up at them. We locked eyes for a brief second.

"Do you have a backpack or some type of bag in your locker man?" One of my classmates asked me.

"Yeah, I got one." I quickly answered.

"Hey man, hey man, I need you to hold on to this until third hour." The upper classmen nervously pulled a nickel plated 38 from the inside pocket of his trench coat.

"Damn," I thought. My heart dropped, and my palms got sweaty.

There was a brief moment of silence between us.

"Alright man," I said. I quickly grabbed my bag before I

quickly reached for the pistol. I carefully placed it underneath my Mathematics workbook after I pulled out my science book in preparation to head to my second hour class. I slowly placed my backpack inside of my locker.

"Naw man...I'm going to meet you outside of your second hour class, go ahead and take the bag with you," He said. I felt my heart beating rapidly as I grabbed my bag, and I slammed my locker door.

I strutted into my science class about five to ten minutes late, and then I sat at least two or three seats from the door after I placed my bag underneath my seat. I looked at the chalkboard, I observed the sloppy written words on it for a moment before I followed their instructions. I looked around the classroom for a moment before I opened my science book, and I begin to read along with the other students. About a minute had passed before my second hour teacher quickly walked passed me to address someone at our classroom door. It was our Vice Principal Mrs. Malone, they stood there chatting for a brief moment. It was silence in the midst of our class room.

"Mr. Dixon, can I speak with you for a moment," She said softly. My heart dropped to my stomach, I felt it thumping rapidly. Damn, I thought.

"Where's the gun?" She asked me. It was a stern look on her face.

"Hun?" I answered. I looked puzzled, I was trying to play it off.

"I already know about the gun," She said.

"Where's your bag?" She asked me.

I dropped my head in disgust before I pointed towards the bottom of my desk. I was embarrassed as I stood there, I was nervous while I watched her remove the weapon from my bag.

"Now what is this?" She asked me. It was a mean mug on her face.

I knew exactly what time it was, my legs wobbled like jello as I followed her to her office. I sat, and I listened to her in silence while she explained what had happened to my Grandma. She looked at me after she hung up the phone. She said, "Don't you know that I could expel you for the rest of the school year, what were you thinking Mr. DIxon?" She asked me. "But, since I already know what happen, and since this is your first time getting into any trouble, I'm only going to suspend you for one day along with three days of In School

Suspension (I.S.S.)."

"Thank you Mrs. Malone," I blurted.

"If you're going to do something wrong, do it by yourself, because you can't tell on yourself." The wise words of my GrandDaddy lingered in my mind as I laid in silence. I gazed at the sand blasted ceiling in my bedroom, my eyes shifted from wall to wall while my mind raced. I was deep in thought.

"When you grow up you're going to be just like your Momma and your Daddy, you're going to be a jailbird." The other kids use to say that whenever they teased me. I felt numb as I laid there, I felt pain as I digest those words, and I felt cursed as I struggled to eliminate that thought. I shut my eyes, I tried to visualize my Father, and I tried to force those words out of my head.

"Fuck them, I ain't going to jail." I mumbled to myself. They burned bread on me, they jinxed me. It was only two weeks after I mumbled those words that I caught my first case. It was on a balmy saturday morning when my homeboy and I got arrested after we beat up another youngster in the neighborhood.

I sat in silence for several hours after my homeboy's Momma came and she picked him up from the Detention Center on 27th and Cherry, my Grandmother showed up to get me moments before the officers' were getting ready to take me to the back to dress me out.

It was a stern look on my Grandma's face when she told me, "This is the first time, and this is the last time that I'll be coming to get you ass out of anybody's jail, I've been through enough of that shit with your Mother and your Uncle's, and I'll be damn if I have to go through that shit with you."

"It won't happen again Grandma," I said during our conversation on the way back home.

It was a cold fall November evening, we were going into the second semester of my Freshman year in High School. The night fell upon us as we rolled through the neighborhood of Lenexa, KS. five deep. I felt the cold air that breezed through the broken window against my face as we turned the corners of the blocks in the small city in search of another automobile to steal. We slowly pulled up beside an Ninety-Eight Oldsmobile because those cars were easier to steal. We watched in silence as one of the homeboys quickly hopped out with his screwdriver in his hand, he quickly popped the glass of the back window then he hopped in it, and he attempted to breakdown the steering wheel. The porch light came on, he hopped back into the car, and we sped off. We quickly turned corner after corner, we quickly searched for an exit to the Highway.

It was right before we reached the exit to the Highway that we sped passed the town Sheriff who had made a quick u-turn and begin to follow us in pursuit. He hit his sirens, but it wasn't no stopping us, we hit the Highway full speed ahead with the town Sheriff hot on our tail.

We were in a high speed chase from Lenexa, KS., we hit the Highway during rush hour traffic with several police cruisers chasing us before the driver use the tire changing lane to speed passed the rush hour traffic, and he shook off the trail of police cruisers that chased us.

We were met by the (KCPD) Kansas City Police Department when we reached Troost, we sped down Troost until we reached 75th Street, we bent the corner of 75th street, we hopped out, and we hit a fence. The high speed chase turned into a foot chase with the Ghetto bird above hovering over us as we ran from the law. I notice an Officer hit a close line before I hopped the fence on Gregory. I was met by several Police cruisers, It was several officers that rushed towards me with their guns drew, they had roughed me up, right before they cuffed me up, and then they threw me in the back of the paddy wagon.

It happened again, it didn't happen immediately, but It happened two years laters. I was fourteen years old when I was arrested for auto theft, but the charge was reduced to tampering.

I evolved into a criminal, I was molded to be a B.G., I was introduced to the dope game, and I entered into the dope game shortly after my introduction. I became a lookout at one of the town's local bud spots on 39th & Jackson. I stood on the corner of 39th & Jackson, and I looked out for the police everyday after I got out of school. I took the money that I was paid for being a lookout, and I went and I bought a double up. I begin to deal drugs, I started to sale crack cocaine.

It was three of my homeboys and me, we were on the set, I was in a rap group called "The Set" back then. I had busted a previously recorded song while we sat on the stairs on 19th street.

"It's the set, it's the set, no sweat claim yo set," I said when I saw one of the neighborhood serves hit the corner. I stood and I walked towards him with my work in my hand.

"What you trying to do?" I asked him. "Give me a dime," He said.

"I'll be back, I got some people coming through later," He told me after I served him.

It was right after I served him that I saw a group of guys from Blue Valley come from over the hill dressed in all blue. One of them had a blue rag tied around his neck, and he wore a pair of loc sunglasses.

"What's up Cuz?" He shouted.

"What be real, Blood?" I shouted back.

The funk was on, they came through the block set tripping. The homies and I approached them shouting our gang slang, they shouted back as we formed a circle, it was time to bang. It was time for one gang member from our group to knuckle up with one gang member from their group in the middle of the circle.

"What's up Blood," I said after I threw up my hands.

"You already know what's up Cuz," He said after he stepped up, but before anyone could throw a punch, the police hit the block, and everybody broke out.

In my community, the youth went from running through the fields with a football to running through the fields with a pocket full of rocks, and a pistol. It became a chaotic environment. We went from challenging each other playing football and basketball, to challenging one another in gang disputes, colors had segregated our community, and colors produced gang violence throughout the community. The fist fights turned into gun battles, and we were blessed that those gun battles didn't turn into any casualties.

Tragedy struck in my life, I suddenly become ill. I suffered from two weeks of constant migraine headaches. The doctor's told my Grandmother that it was a sinus infection, they prescribed several medications, but they didn't work.

I sat in my first hour class, my head pounded, it thumped constantly, and my mouth watered. I swallowed a mouthful of spit before I raised my hand to address the teacher. When he called on me, I tried to speak, but I couldn't, no words would come out of my mouth. I mumbled when I tried to tell him that I wasn't feeling good. He contacted the security guard who took me down to the principal's office to call my Grandmother.

She arrived ten minutes later, fifth-teen minutes later we arrived at the hospital, it was thirty minutes after we arrived at the hospital that I had blacked out. I drifted in and out as the nurses and the doctors scrambled to see what was wrong with me. I had a stroke at the age of sixteen, and I went into a coma. I was rushed to Research Medical Center to have an emergency brain surgery. I woke up three days later with two tubes hanging out of my head.

I had to learn how to talk again, and I had to learn how to walk again, I had to go to physical therapy for six months, I had home school for the duration of the school year with an around the clock nurse that came to give me medicine through an IV, I had eight months to a year of constant therapy, and I had a year of constant doctor's visits. Everyone told me that they thought that they had lost me, anyone would have thought that this would've been a life changing event, but it wasn't.

I didn't want to get involved into anything positive, I was

influenced by negative things. My Grandmother tried to steer me towards several opportunities that she had lined up for me, such as; enrolling me in Barber College after I graduated, but I decided to go in another direction.

I started back smoking weed while I was taking my medication, and it wasn't long before I had my first experience with PCP at the age of seventeen. I smoked PCP mixed with marijuana, we called it Lovely. I was influenced by the peer pressure, and I was heavily under the influence of a controlled substance, I was influenced by the trend of smoking marijuana. I stayed on cloud nine, and my drug use progressed to using harder drugs like PCP. I felt trapped, I felt confined, the hood took me under, and I continued to dig myself deeper into a bottomless pit.

I started back dealing drugs at the beginning of my senior year in high school. I sold crack cocaine, and I sold a lot of it. I dropped out of high school to become a full time dopeman. I became obsessed with that lifestyle, I became addicted to alcohol and drugs, and I became addicted to the fast money that came along with the sale of them.

I had been in various shoot outs, I had multiple run ins with the law, and I had also recorded a hit song called "The Dank Session" on the KRO album by the age of eighteen. It was also the year that I got shot, I got shot twice, once in both of my legs.

I laid in silence with my bandaged legs propped up onto several pillows. I stared at the sand blasted ceiling in my bedroom with thoughts of retaliation running through my mind. I begin to reason with myself after replaying that cold night over and over again in my mind, I begin to listen to that small voice in my head. It was like God was trying to get my attention, and this time I listened to him. I closed my eyes, and I said a quick prayer. My thoughts changed instantly, they went from being vindictive to being productive. I took a quick glance at the muted television, and I noticed a commercial that advertised Excelsior Springs Job Corps. I reached for the inkpen, and a piece of paper that sat on top of a shelf at the head of my bed, and I quickly jotted down the number.

I made a split decision to continue my education. The next day I called and I spoke with a job corp placement recruiter. I pondered a new beginning, I thought of what life would be like if I finished my education, and I thought of how life would be if I worked a steady job instead of dealing drugs. I enrolled in Job Corp, and I started to acquire a trade while I studied towards obtaining my GED. I attended trade one week, and I attended education the next week, I alternated from week to week for nine months. It was an informative nine months, and it was an educational nine months. I received a pay allotment every two weeks, I received $30 every two weeks, they gave me $21 of it, and they put the rest into a savings account for me.

It was a sunny Saturday on September 23, 1996. It was a bus full of students, we rode from Excelsior Springs to Maple Woods College, we were heading to the college to take our GED test. Everyone listened to the sounds of Hot 103.3 Jamz as we rode, several students song along with the songs that played. It was during a commercial break that everyone received the disturbing news. I went to take my GED on the same day that Tupac Shakur was pronounced dead.

I walked across the stage in my cap and my gown on November 15, 1996. It felt amazing to finally accomplish something, it felt wonderful to see the smile on my Grandmother's face when I handed her my certificates.

She asked me, "So; what are your plans, what are you going to do now?"

"I'm going to advanced training for HVAC, or to the Navy Reserves Grandma," I said.

I took the test for the reserves, and I failed. I looked into advanced training in Atlanta for HVAC, but I didn't follow through with that. I gave up, my vision was off, I didn't contact the job recruiter that could of linked me up with a job that would able me to utilize my skills that I learned.

I took the money that I saved in Job Corp and I bought some dope to flip. I ended up back on the block hustling. I felt like that was my only other option, I felt like I had tried everything else, but I really didn't put forth any effort. I expected to be rewarded for things that other young people done without any hesitation, I wanted to be catered to, I wanted something for nothing, and that's what I did, I went out there, and I chased after something for a little bit of nothing.

I observed the white rocked up substance that I held onto loosely before I dropped it into the hands of one of my customers. I gave him the last of what I had, I threw him a bump for a little bit of nothing, he gave me two dollars for a dime.

The sun was going down, it was hidden behind the clouds as it eased through the horizon. I was on the block posted, I been out there all day, I waited impatiently for some money to arrive. I stood at the edge of the stairs smoking a blunt looking down at the debris that polluted the block. I took a puff of the blunt before I looked up, I noticed a serve heading in my direction, he was looking for something.

"Yee!"

He looked in my direction before he doubled back, and he headed my way. I watched him as he swiftly paced towards me. I stood at the edge of the curve when he arrived.

"What's up, what you looking for?" I asked him. "I need a dime," He said.

"I got a couple of dollars in change, go ahead and work with me youngster, and I'll bring some more money yo way."

I waited anxiously for my work to arrive, it was considered to be some of the best work in the hood. I gave a neighborhood customer a tester, he was one of the hoods loyal serves, he spent money everyday. I wanted him to run me some more money after I got back on, I got him started, I got him to run me serves.

He bought the little bit of dope that I had left, and he had more money coming through. I was on the edge, I needed to re-up, and I needed some more dope pronto.

I gripped the safety pin before I grabbed the dope, I cut it into small chunks, I tossed the chunks into the corner of a sandwich bag, and I tied it into a knot. I repeated that process for several minutes until I had a bag full of dope. I quickly reached for my pager, I yanked it off of my hip as it vibrated rapidly. I glanced at it for a moment, and I smiled. It was my runner, he wanted three for fifty.

The projects was checking, the hood was jumping, I was moving fast, and I was making money. I had came up, I had fell off, and I had came back up again. It was during this time in my life that I hit the studio, and I recorded a song with the homies from the hood called "The Projects Be Checking," featuring Messy Marv, we collaborated on the Twamp Side album. It was also during this time in my life that I had caught my first dope case.

It was high noon, it was on a Saturday, and I had just left the corner store with a 24oz can of Bud Ice and a pack of Swisher Sweet cigars in a paper sack, I grip the sack tightly before I jogged across the street. I was in a hurry, I quickly walked down 17th St., I was headed to a concert that evening, but before I left to get ready for the night I decided to smoke a blunt and drink a brew with the homies. I hit the block, and I linked up with the fellows, I rolled up a blunt, and we begin to do our thing. I noticed a police car parked at the end of the block. I tried to play it off before I told the Homies, "There go them boys." I saw another police cruiser quickly pull up behind him. I tightly clinched the blunt that I held before I swiftly threw it across the grass as I swiftly walked down the street. It was right after I had tossed the blunt that the police officer hit his sirens as he eased up on us. "Fuck," I whispered to myself before I stopped, and I followed behind the homies, and I walked towards the edge of the curb. It was two police officers that stepped out of each vehicle. They directed us towards the hood of the car, it was two officers that had pat us down while the other two officers had searched the area. It was a few minutes later that one of the officer's had frisked me. He swiftly patted me down before he removed a bankroll from my back pocket, and then he put me in handcuffs. He said, "Mr. Dixon you're under arrest for the possession of a controlled substance. I dropped my head in disbelief before he put me in the back seat of the police cruiser. He dangled a bag full of rocks in front of me. "Fuck Naw!, that shit ain't mine!" I yelled.

It wasn't long before I was back at it, and it wasn't long before I caught another dope case, I caught dope case after dope case, I caught a total of three dope cases. I got a good lawyer, I paid him fifth-teen hundred dollars, and I got placed on three years probation.

I continued to bump my head against a stone wall, I lived a young life full of ups and downs, I lived my young life on a merry go round. I violated my probation after I dropped a dirty UA. I was stipulated to attend drug classes every Tuesday, but I caught another dope case, and my probation was revoked.

I had just turned twenty two years old, and I got locked up two weeks after my birthday.   I sat in the county jail for four months that was around the time that I received the bad news about my little brother, he had got locked up two weeks before his birthday. He was charged with Second Degree Assault and Attempted Murder after he was accused of shooting two Police officers on New Year's Eve, those chain of events happened at least a year after several police officers had shot and, they had killed Timothy Wilson may he (R.I.P.). I was tired of eluding the law, I tired of scheming and plotting, and I was tired of constantly looking over my shoulder, I was tired of worrying about getting shot down by the police, or being robbed and killed by some player hater. This was the turning point in my life, I called my public defender, and I told him that I was prepared to accept the offer that was on the table. The court had offered me eight years for Drug trafficking in the 2nd degree, an additional eight years for another Drug Trafficking charge, and seven years for Drug Possession, all to run concurrent.

    I sat in silence, and I listened to the other inmates that were in the holding tank getting ready to pull chain. It was the first thing in the morning, it was about 7:00 O'clock in the morning, we just finished eating breakfast before they gave us all a sack lunch. We sat in the holding tank for at least a hour and a half before several officers arrived with multiple sets of handcuffs, they cuffed us up one inmate at a time, they placed the handcuffs on my wrist, and then they placed a set of handcuffs on my ankles before they escorted us out to the Grey Goose, we all walked in a single file line before we boarded the bus. We rode in silence, we arrived in St. Joseph Missouri forty-five minutes later.

I was sent to prison on January 28, 2000 to serve an eight year bid at the age of twenty two years old.

It was approximately fifty inmates, we had sat in two holding tanks while we waited to be processed with R&O, we sat side by side, we sat there naked with a bath towels around our waist, and we were called in one by one, each offender was sprayed down with lice spray before we were sent through the shower, after we hit the shower, we were sent to laundry to get our clothing, and our bedding items along with a (P&P) Probation and Parole booklet before we were called in one by one to inmate registration. It was after everyone was registered that we all were given sack lunches, and we were escorted around to our housing units.

I was escorted to housing unit one after serving a month in the diagnostic center. I had seen Probation and Parole prior to hitting the hill, and I was stipulated to a 180 day treatment program, I felt like I had a chance to get back to life as I walked to my housing unit. I had begin to have that talk with myself as we approached the aging housing unit. I had told myself that I could get through this, and I had told myself that I should keep to myself, and keep gangster as I usually do.

It was September the fourth of 2000, It was my birthday. I had sat at a table in the public area of our housing unit with a plate of Nacho's and a cup of peach twist in front of me, it was me and three other inmates at the table, one of them had quickly shuffled a deck of cards before he dealt them. The evening news was on, I glanced at the television,and I noticed that my neighborhood was in the headlines once again. I focused in on what happened in the hood, it was a murder that had took place on the day of my birthday. It was the senseless murder of my little homie name George (R.I.P), I had known him ever since he was a child, I watched him grow up. I was devastated, I was crushed after I found out that I had lost one of my childhood friends one week before George was murdered, some one had the audacity to kill my other homie Ree tha Hogg (R.I.P). I became unwilling to compromise with the Correctional officers after a beef with another inmate from a rival gang. I was placed in the hole, and I was transferred to another prison.

I had lost my 180 day treatment, and I had to serve my time. I did the crime, so I had to do my time, and that's what I did. I did it minute after minute, hour after hour, day after day, month after month, and calendar after calendar.

While I was incarcerated I read book after book, and I worked out everyday. I planned to be physically and mentally prepared for life on the outside. I can remember the frustration that I felt during mail call, I can remember the disappointment that I felt every time my celly got called out for a visit, and I can recall the times that I didn't have any money on my books, those were painful moments during my bid. I decided to do something constructive, I got put up on game by my OG celly. I had filed my taxes from previous years of work, and I sent a seven dollar green check to the Missouri Secretary of State for a fictitious name registration for a business called Down & Dirty Productions. I took up a trade, and I obtained a plumbing certificate while I was incarcerated, and I also attended NA every week. I served two years in prison before I went to go see the parole board, and they gave me a fourteen month out date. I signed up for the work release program, and I was moved to Housing Unit 10 after they accepted my application. I was assigned to the MODOT Crew, we were transported to the inner city to pick up trash on the Highway. I worked on the work release crew for ten months before I was released from prison. I got released from prison on January 28, 2003.

When I was getting out, my little brother was going in, he was sentenced to four life sentences plus sixty years for his crime, I was devastated, I was disappointed that he wouldn't be there when I got home.

I rode in silence in the presence of my Uncle, and my Grandma. We had spent a little time together before they took me to the Kansas City Community Release Center KCCRC, but everyone calls it The Honor Center. I walked in the Honor Center with a little pocket change, and my walking papers. I quickly settled in, I went through orientation, I saw my P.O., I received my stipulations, and I was out on a the job search. I can remember how it felt standing in those long lines waiting to get out to make appointments and interviews on time that

was a humbling experience. I got out on my job search, and I applied at Gates BBQ on 12th & Brooklyn, and I got hired the same day. I was on the block, but I was on a different block, I was on the chopping block at Gates Barbecue. It felt good because I was working, I felt good because I was doing something positive, it felt good because I was doing my thing. I had two weeks on the job, It was somewhere around February 12th 2003, it was on the same day of my big homies' birthday may he (Rest In Peace). It was a light snow that light snow had turned into a heavy snow that's when 6-4 walked through the door. I greeted him, "What's up big homie," I said after I gave him a quick hug and a handshake. He order a mix plate after he jotted down his phone number right before he walked out of the door he said, "Call me Kool Breeze."
It had got slow and my supervisor had let me off work early, I had a little bit of room to play, I had enough time to spend on the reservations that I made for Marijane and Remy. I called 6-4, he came, and he scooped me up. He was ready to celebrate, he handed me a fifth of Remy before He said, "What's up Kool Breeze, I'm glad to see you back out on the bricks, what you want to do tonight? It's my birthday." I said,

"You know what 6-4 man, out of my twenty-four years of life, I've never been to a strip club. "Say no more," He said as he slowly turned the corner, we ended up over the homies house moments later.

I was on my 2nd or 3rd cup of Remy, I was bustin rhymes that I wrote while I was down, we were kicking it, we were doing our thing. It was big blunts going around, it was good smoke in the air. I already had reservations, Fuck it, I thought. I took a couple of puffs of the blunt, and I got into rotation, we smoked three blunts before we headed out to the strip club, we hit another spot after we left that club, time had elapsed, and I didn't get in until 5 o'clock in the morning.

I was four hours late, and I was intoxicated. They breathalyzed me, and they gave me a UA before they sent me to my room. I saw my P.O the next day, and I was placed on two weeks building restriction. I lost my job at Gates, but I didn't give up. I found another job at Mr. Goodcents downtown.

I went to see my grandfather one day after work, and that was the last time that I saw him alive, shortly after our visit he had a heart attack. I still remember the last conversation that we had, He said, "I know that you're frustrated, but just make sure that you don't kill nobody."

I struggled emotionally, I was having a hard time dealing with the loss of my Grandfather. His words lingered in my mind while I was at work. I went to work early on the day of his funeral, and I asked my supervisor if I could attend my grandfather's funeral. He gave me permission, He said that I can go to the viewing of his body, but I couldn't go to the grave site. He said, I could go, but I had to be back by One o'clock. I had to honor that because I was already in trouble, I was already skating on thin ice. I got back at 1 o'clock, and I worked to the end of my shift, at the end of the day the man calls me into his office, and he tells me that I was fired. I was enraged, my eyes shifted from him to the safe. I didn't even get a chance to see where my Grandfather was buried. I cussed, and I fussed with tears in my eyes as I walked back around to the community release center. I stopped in mid stride, I through up hands, and I said f*** it. I needed a drink, I needed something to smoke, and I needed to self medicate. The death of my Grandfather was what triggered my need to drink and drug. I called one of my homeboys, we linked up, and we turned up. I found relief at the bottom of a bottle. I ended up staying out all night, and when I got back they put me in the hole. I stayed in the hole for about a week after they teamed me on my violation before they had rolled me back to St. Joe.

I can remember the dull process of going through St. Joe Diagnostic Center. I thought that I'd never have to go through that again, I thought that I would never have to sit naked on that cold concrete while waiting to shower, I thought that I would never have to get sprayed down with lice spray again, but I did. I had to endure that dull process once again.

I went to see the parole board five weeks later, and I was stipulated to the 84 and out treatment program. I would be released back into society on parole after 84 days of successful programming. I was sent to Fulton, Missouri where I begin my treatment. It was an intense environment, and it was a structured environment. I sat in a circle of other alcoholics and addicts who also had a problem with alcohol and drugs. I browsed the circle of men as they introduced themselves before I said, "I'm Deontae, and I'm addicted to fast money, marijuana, and alcohol."

We had to do our homework assignments, we had to shave everyday, and we had to work the 12 steps program. It was during this process that I had got the nuts and bolts of the program, it was during this process that I learned the program and how it works, and it works if you work it. It was during this process that I finally realized that I had a problem. That's when I had admitted that I was powerless over my addiction, and that my life had become unmanageable. I had to admit that after I had calculated the amount of money that I wasted on drinks, and all of the money that I spent on drugs in a day. It was humiliating to me, it was discouraging to me, it was frustrating for me to know that I had hustled so hard, that I had worked so hard, and that I didn't have anything to show for it. There were moments during the program, and there were times throughout my prison stretch that I didn't even have cigarettes. I felt ashamed of myself, but I didn't waddle in self-pity, I had to pick myself up, and I had to dust myself off.

I worked my treatment program, I learned that 90% of communication is listening, I had to close my mouth, and I had to open my ears to listen. I took a good look around me, and I opened my eyes to observe life clearly.

I finally got through the 84 day program, and I graduated. I was scheduled for release, but I had to stay there for an additional week because I didn't have a home plan. The Honor Center was packed, and the HalfWay House had a two month waiting list. The only other option that I had was to go to the Dismas House in St. Louis, I snatched that up. I was frustrated because it felt like I didn't have anyone. I begin to place blame on others, I shifted the blame, I was in denial, but I realized that I must become accountable for actions. I became more aware of my thoughts, I became more aware of my words, and my actions. I had to let go of resentments because harboring resentments only fueled my anger.

I got out on August 15, 2003, I touched down in St. Louis. I'll never forget it, I'll never forget how gutter St. Louis was. I got there on a sunny afternoon, I remember the moment when I hit the Greyhound Station, I still remember the cab driver. He had took me to the Dismas House off of Kings Highway & Martin Luther King. I stepped in there, and I began to adapt to another environment. It wasn't easy for me to stay optimistic because all I had was my walking papers, my state greys, and my afro pick. I was fortunate enough to find a few pieces of clothing, and a pair of tennis shoes.

I hit the track running the next day, I was out to work. I spent the last couple of dollars that I had, and I caught the Saint Charles n Rock Road bus down to Saint Charles n Rock Road over in Weston, and I hit the temporary service. I ended up landing a two week assignment, and I put a few dollars in my pocket I begin to meet people, I started shaking hands with other criminals, I was on the prowl, but I did my own thing.

I turned 26 years old in St Louis, and it was a beautiful 26 because I was clean and I sober.

I started to celebrate, I started back smoking weed two or three weeks after my birthday. I was slipping through the cracks, and I wasn't sticking out like a sore thumb. I realize that the treatment facilitator was right, when she said, "Always try do the right thing when no one is looking."

I found another job working from 7 p.m to 7 a.m at a local WalMart after that temporary assignment was over.

I saved some money, and I moved out of the Dismas House, I moved into an apartment building that rented rooms for $75 a week on Clemons, it was three blocks off of Delmar.

It was on a quiet monotonous Thanksgiving that I wanted to be around family. I decided to pack my bags, and I decided to catch the bus down to the Greyhound station. It was a hairsplitting decision, It was just like I was catching the bus to the grocery store. I had just got paid, and I had went home to be with family for the holiday.

I arrived in Kansas City a little bit after dinner time, it was around seven o'clock when I popped up on my Grandmother. She wasn't expecting me, she was surprised to see me after she buzzed me in. "I thought you was in St. Louis," She said after she hugged me, and she gave me a kiss on the cheek. I eat Thanksgiving dinner, and I sat and talk with my GrandMother. I had told her how good things were going for me in St. Louis.

In the midst of me being in KC for the holiday's, I became stuck in KC after the holidays. My alcohol use, and my drug use had progressed. I had spent the money that I had for my bus ticket back to St. Louis, I had spent it on drink and drugs. I was being irresponsible once again. I called in to work, and I eventually quit my job. I slip backwards, I went back to my old ways. I craved fast money, I had an appetite for paper can you savor the flavor, I was money hungry, and I wanted more. I abscond on parole, I was on the run for about eight months. I was going back and forth to St. Louis for a while before I finally decided to turn myself in. My P.O directed me towards the Honor Center where I sat in the hole for a week before I was shipped back to St. Joe.

I had to endure that dull process once again, I had to get sprayed down with the lice spray once again, and I had to go to see P & P once again. I had got used to that, I was becoming a career criminal. That's when I realized that those were just revolving doors, and I realized that I was just another number.

I begin to reason with myself, I told myself that I got to do this, I told myself that I have to muster up the strength to handle things emotionally, I told myself that I had to handle those frustrations without using drink or drugs while I was under the stipulation of parole. I was addicted to what we call the gateway drug which is marijuana, I love maryjane.

I got sent back to Fulton, Missouri to complete another treatment program. It was a 30 day program, it was 30 days and out. I had started to notice my characters defects, I had that thing that we spoke of in treatment called codependency, and I suffered from depression. I realized that it was only a power that was greater than myself that could restore me to sanity. I made my mind up, I was sick and tired of being sick and tired. I made a decision to turn my will and my life over to the care of God as I understood him, and I made a searching and fearless inventory of myself before I completed the 30 day and out program.

I was released back into society without any immediate or short term goals, I had tunnel vision. They say you should have a plan or plan to fail, and that's what I did. I failed after giving the clean and sober life a try, I had fail once again, but I wasn't giving up. I admitted to God, to myself, and to another human being the exact nature of my wrongs.

I had contacted my P.O after I had been forced out of an unhealthy relationship. I was entirely ready to have God remove all of those defects of character. My P.O directed me towards a Treatment Center, it was a place where I could redirect my focus after I detoxed, after I detoxed I entered into a treatment program for twenty-one days. I sobered up, and I moved into a Transitional Living Center, it was a place that keeps a person off of the streets, it was a place of refuge. I went through an outpatient treatment before I found a job, after I found a job, I found a spot. I transition back into society, but I wasn't done, I still had reservations.

I relapsed, I started back smoking, but it wasn't marijuana, it was PCP, marijuana was the gateway drug that cause me to start back smoking PCP. I lost my grip on life, I lost my job, and I lost my house.

I had become mentally ill, I had suffered from a compulsive obsessive disorder called alcoholism and drug abuse. It was back through the transitional living process, it was back to outpatient once again. I had went through detox, and I had been through treatment at least 10 to 12 times by this time in my life.

I was getting ready to be released from parole, I had about 8 months left on parole at 28 years old. I had humbly asked God to remove my shortcomings.

"A winner never quits, and a quitter never wins."

I was reunited with my father at the age of 30 years old, after I was released from parole.

I rode in silence on the Greyhound bus. We went through

Kansas first, then it was through Arlington, Texas, to New Mexico, to Utah, and through Vegas until we finally reached California.

It felt amazing to be in a new location, I felt relieved, and I felt refreshed. I had a new beginning, I had a new start, and I was excited about being reunited with my father.

I begin the pre-production of my first novel, my first book titled the Inspirations of a Young Black Pimp after I filed a form 2643, and a DBA name registration for a company called Down & Dirty Publishing one month after being released from parole. I had plans to run a book & magazine publishing house once I was released from prison. I begin to make contacts with music industry professionals after I filed a DBA name registration for a Music Publishing Company called Prosedz Publishing, I also had plans to enter the music industry once I was released from prison. I begin to make deals on my own, I got in touch with an indie distribution company that has connects with over twenty-five thousand chain retail stores for my music, and I contacted an indie book publishing company about the replication of my first book. I was making preparations to put my business plan in motion.

I sent a short form PA to the Library of Congress along with a typed copy of my lyrics before I joined (ASCAP) the American Society of Composers Authors and Publishers. I planned to get paid by the minute, instead of being paid by the hour.

I found a job, and I begin to work towards my goals. I worked several jobs, I worked at Quality Inn on South H, I had the opportunity to go out to Tehachapi, California to work in the oil fields, and I worked at a MDS Communication's on Stockdale Highway. I love Cali, California has a lot of opportunities.

I begin to meet people, I begin to socialize, I mixed and mingled with my step brothers in Fresno smoking indo, we went to a couple of clubs, we hit a couple of spots in Bakersfield. My father has a wonderful family out there, he has a beautiful wife, three step sons, and a step daughter that he helped raise as his own. I stayed out there for 8 months. I got everything together, I put together a little bit of pocket change, and I headed back to Kansas City.

I got back to Kansas City on Memorials Day, as soon as I got here, I regret leaving California, but I did because I wanted to be closer to home. My grandmother was getting older, and it was about time for moms to get out of prison.

It was raining when I got to Kansas City, and I didn't have a place to stay. I decided to go in the right direction instead of being out in the streets, rippin and runnin the streets doing the wrong things with the wrong people. I had vowed to never touch another crumb of crack again, I didn't want to go back to dealing drugs. "A man must stand for something or he will fall for anything." It was important for me to stand solid on my own two feet instead of being co-dependent of anyone. I moved back into another Transitional Living spot, and I made a list of all persons I had harmed, and I became willing to make amends to them all. I made direct amends to such people whenever possible, except when to do so would injure them or others. I wanted to make up for lost time, I needed to make things right with my Grandmother, and I did before I made another successful transition back into society eight months later after I found another job. I had became the Ice Cream Man.

I was faced with the responsibilities that required me to perform on a level of excellence because I was an independent contractor, that means that my paycheck depends on how hard I ring my bell. I had to meet the demands of the market that called for me adapt and then I could eventually evolve into the man that I was intended to be, an Independent Publisher, Author, and Artist. I had to become accountable, and I had to become dependable. I was required to be a man of my word, and I was required to be about my business. I had to sharpen those characteristics, and I had to tighten up those abilities that pushed me towards success. I'm a man that has perfected his craft, and I enjoy what I do for a living. I have the opportunity to turn my hobby into a career.

I now realize that to excel at what I do, it requires self-awareness and daily inventory, but after taking a close observation of myself I begin to feel void. I feel that way at times because, I know where I've been, I'm focused on where I'm trying to go, but I'm uncertain about all the bullshit that's along the way. I feel empty at times because I'm giving it all that I got. That's the purpose of my book; titled: Frustrated "Thoughts Becoming Words." I choose to name my Autobiography Frustrated "Thoughts Becoming Words," because writing this gave me the opportunity to release some steam, writing this gives me a direct outlet for my negative energy, and it gives me a postive way to deal with my frustration.

I instantly became overwhelmed with thoughts of my life when I started this project. I thought of all of my failures in an instant, memories of the times that I have procrastinated, and thoughts of me prolonging the gratification of obtaining my goals ran through my mind. I had begin to feel discontent, I realized that my life has not been that extraordinary after I continued to take personal inventory of myself, and when I was wrong, I promptly admitted it.

I sat in my ice cream truck on that summer afternoon, I briefly inventoried my demeanor, and I quickly observed my outlook on things.

I sat there for a moment, and I stared out of the window. I released a stressful sigh before I started my truck. I sorted through my cooler, and I grabbed a bottle of water, It was hot, and I needed to cool off. The temperature had risen at least ten degrees. I turned on the fan that was mounted on the edge of the ceiling, I was seeking relief from the summer heat. I prepared myself for a long day, I was getting ready to drive along my route.

I actually enjoyed what I did for a living during that time in my life because I had the freedom to operate how I wanted to. I would buy packages of suckers, and I would give them away to the children that didn't have any money to buy ice cream. I became familiar with my sales territory and also my customers.

I quickly glanced downward at the clock that was inside of the front panel of my ice cream truck, I turned up the radio after I made a right turn on 27t h Street. I pressed the peddle to the metal. I held the urge to smoke a blunt as I headed east towards my neighborhood to buy a sack of weed. I moved through traffic in a hurry because time wasn't on my side on this particular day.

I visualized getting to my first commercial business right on their break time and thought of how everyone usually bought ice cream. I look forward to getting that money which was an anticipated contribution towards my desired sales goal for the day. I was paid thirty five percent off of the money that I made. This means I would get thirty-five dollars off of every one-hundred dollars that I made.

I can see myself making at least four-hundred dollars today, I thought as I shifted through traffic heading east on 23r d and Vanbrunt.

I silently calculated the money that I had already made for that week, I quickly added the one hundred and forty dollars that I would make on that day as I subtracted my gas expenses, and then I deducted the extra five to ten dollars that I held back for lunch or cigarettes on various occasions throughout the week. "Fuck!" I said as I momentarily did the math.

I held thoughts of my habits as I stopped at the red light gazing out at the flow of automobiles that sped past me. I took a quick look at myself in the rearview mirror, I wiped the sweat off of my forehead with a towel that I kept inside of my truck. The reflection of the noon sun shined through the windshield and I could see my pupils dilate. I swiftly placed my Pit Bull ball cap back on top of my head, I neatly slanted it slightly to the left as I slowly eased through the traffic light. I was only blocks away from the community where I grew up. Childhood memories began to surface as I drove pass three young men from the hood that walked down 23r d Street, they gestured with their hands while they walked and talked.

I had visualized myself headed in that same direction many times before as I proceeded. I can remember it as if it were only yesterday. Damn, I thought as I remembered all of the times that my friends and I were headed down that very same path. It was a road that could lead a youngster to self-destruction, or a path that could aid in the construction of an adolescence in their transformation into a curious teen.

There was a still silence as the radio paused for a minute, it was going into a commercial while I waited at the traffic light on Topping Street. I was only one short block away from the weed man. I gazed at the large wooden sign with its green and white paint fading, it was Park Towers back then, but now it promoted Hilltop Townhomes to potential renters on the corner of 23rd Street.

I glanced into Blue Valley Park as I moved along, and I noticed a group of people gathered at the first shelter with their automobiles parked sideways, facing the street.

My feelings of frustration were replaced with feelings of excitement as I briefly reminisced about the days that I would be the man who stood over the barbecue grill with my apron on, and a beer in my hand as the music blasted.

In a flash all of the strife that was associated with my lifestyle crossed my mind as I turned the corner of Wheeling Street, and I entered Blue Valley Court Apartments.

Damn, I thought. I considered the length of time that I've stayed in the hood, I thought of how I aimlessly ripped and I carelessly ran through the streets of Hilltop without a care in the world except for the police.

I eased down the steep hill of Blue Valley. I noticed the leaves swaying in the dry breeze when I looked to the right of me, right before I reached the bottom of the hill. The Metro bus had leisurely cruised past me after I made a left turn, and I entered the second block of the aging projects. Several pieces of trash had blown out into the street from the overflowing garbage dumpster that sat at the end of the block.

I quickly swerved towards the curb to serve a group of children that stood at its edge waving their dollars.

I felt that it was important for me to be patient with the kids in the community, and allow them the opportunity to be good stewards over their money.

"Time is money." I silently thought to myself as I moved swiftly inside my ice cream truck.

I stood hunched over the freezer, and I fumbled with its lock for a moment. I felt a sharp pain at the small of my back as I unlocked the freezer. Seconds later, I was leaning out of the window to take their order. I looked into the bright eyes of my first customer as she browsed the menu clutching her dollar. In order to save a little bit of time, I directed her towards the dollar menu along with the others that stood in line.

"OK... four Bubble Gum bars." I said as I handed each of them their ice cream moments later.

"Thank you, and watch for cars!" I yelled when they ran out into the street, they happily eat their ice creams as they skip along.

I paused for a moment as I watched them go about their way. I briefly glanced at the addresses of the Town Homes in remembrance before I hopped back into the driver's seat. I shifted my truck into drive, I allowed it to slowly move forward as I slowly tapped the gas, and I eased over the speed bump that was placed in the center of the road. I glanced to my left at the apartment where I began to form my memory as a child, it was where we stayed before momma got locked up. I sought through prayer and meditation to improve my conscious contact with God as I understood him, and I prayed only for the knowledge of his will for me, and the power to carry that out as I shifted into reverse, and I parked outside of 6-4's apartment. I listened to the music play while I sat there, and I waited for him to come outside. I lit a cigarette to ease some of the tension that I felt. It was beads of sweat that formed along my nose and my forehead. I grabbed the towel that was laid across the back of my seat, and I wiped my face and my head. I felt as if I wouldn't succeed after I quickly viewed the way that I've been living while I twisted a blunt. I shook my head in silence after I turned down the radio. "That's fucked up!" I said to myself.

 "When will the madness stop?" I thought. Colors had segregated my hood; it was Hilltop against Blue Valley, Quincy St. against Chelsea St., the Bloods against the Crips. "It's been a cruel journey." I thought as I begin to think of my driven purpose.

Attention Ghetto Citizens:

We've been ashamed by the world, we've despised, and we've been rejected. We got set aside, now we reside in the projects where life is hectic. It is where the youth is not expected to live past twenty-one. It's our low income that leaves our families feeling numb because we're living in the slums.

We rise; it's our basic instinct, we were born to survive. When I look my people in the eyes I see pain, but I also see the strength to maintain, these streets are calling my name. I've been persuade to pervade pain for a tax free salary, and I had got confined to a perimeter full of pernicious personalities. We're stressed and depressed, we sell dope to get over in a world that's unjust; oppressed.

Many have been blessed to see success, but they're oppressed by their prejudice. While us Ghetto Children roam the streets and smoke angel dust, we're robbing, we're stealing, we're use to suffering from pain; so we smother our feelings, we're heavy alcohol and drug abusers, dope dealing.

And they say, "We're heading for disaster."

All of the ghetto children sharing laughter who are playing in the projects where we were born bastards.

Let's view the after effects of the kids who has been exposed to neglect, with the lost of self-esteem, and self-respect.

"This is a Reality Check."

It was on July, 25 2013 that I received my reality check, that was the day and the year that my Grandmother had passed away. I can remember the pain that I felt from the lost of my Grandmother, I can remember the disappointment. I had to muster up the strength to carry on, I had to keep my grip on life, I had to keep my vision of leading a productive life after having a spiritual awakening as a result of these steps, and I try to carry this message to other alcoholics and addicts to practice these principles in all of my affairs.

I made some sudden changes, It was shortly after the lost of my Grandmother that my Mother was released from prison after serving thirty long years. I can't explain how amazing it felt to finally hug my Mother when I saw her.

Life is life, and I'm living life on life's terms, I'm leading my life one moment at time, I'm living my life one step at a time, and I put my best foot forward in my new walk of life. I decided to take the road that's less traveled, it's a narrow road on a straight path.

God grant me the serenity to accept the things that I can not change, the courage to change the things that I can, and the wisdom to know the difference, God's will not mine be done. Amen

The 12 Steps of Alcoholics Anonymous

1. We admitted we were powerless over alcohol - that our lives had become unmanageable.

2. Came to believe that a Power greater than ourselves could restore us to sanity.

3. Made a decision to turn our will and our lives over to the care of God as we understood Him.

4. Made a searching and fearless moral inventory of ourselves.

5. Admitted to God, to ourselves and to another human being the exact nature of our wrongs.

6. Were entirely ready to have God remove all these defects of character.

7. Humbly asked Him to remove our shortcomings.

8. Made a list of all persons we had harmed, and became willing to make amends to them all.

9. Made direct amends to such people wherever possible, except when to do so would injure them or others.

10. Continued to take personal inventory and when we were wrong promptly admitted it.

11. Sought through prayer and meditation to improve our conscious contact with God as we understood Him, praying

only for knowledge of His will for us and the power to carry that out.

12. Having had a spiritual awakening as the result of these steps, we tried to carry this message to other alcoholics and addicts to practice these principles in all our affairs.

Thank You, Sincerely Deontae Dixon

Time Management Worksheet Provided by corporatetrainingmaterials.com

Goal setting is critical to effective time management strategies. It is the single most important life skill that, unfortunately, most people never learn how to do properly. Goal setting can be used in every single area of your life, including financial, physical, personal development, relationships, or even spiritual. According to Brian Tracy's book Goals, fewer than 3% of people have clear, written goals, and a plan for getting there. Setting goals puts you ahead of the pack!

Some people blame everything that goes wrong in their life on something or someone else. They take the role of a victim and they give all their power and control away. Successful people instead dedicate themselves towards taking responsibility for their lives, no matter what the unforeseen or uncontrollable events. Live in the present: the past cannot be changed, and the future is the direct result of what you do right now!

The Three P's

Setting meaningful, long-term goals is a giant step toward achieving your dreams. In turn, setting and achieving short-term goals can help you accomplish the tasks you'll need to achieve the long-term ones. It is also important to make sure that all of your goals unleash the power of the three P's:

POSITIVE : Who could get fired up about a goal such as "Find a career that's not boring"? Goals should be phrased positively, so they help you feel good about yourself and what you're trying to accomplish. A better alternative might be this: "Enroll in pre-law classes so I can help people with legal problems someday."

PERSONAL : Goals must be personal. They must reflect your own dreams and values, not those of friends, family, or the media. When crafting your goal statement, always use the word "I" in the sentence to brand it as your own. When your goals are personal, you'll be more motivated to succeed and take greater pride in your accomplishments.

POSSIBLE : When setting goals, be sure to consider what's possible and within your control. Getting into an Ivy League university may be possible if you are earning good grades but unrealistic if you're struggling. In the latter case, a more reasonable goal might be to attend a university or trade school that offers courses related to your chosen career. You might also pursue volunteer work that would strengthen your college applications.

The SMART Way

SMART is a convenient acronym for the set of criteria that a goal must have in order for it to be realized by the goal achiever.

Specific : Success coach Jack Canfield states in his book The Success Principles that, "Vague goals produce vague results." In order for you to achieve a goal, you must be very clear about what exactly you want. Often creating a list of benefits that the accomplishment of your goal will bring to your life, will give your mind a compelling reason to pursue that goal.

Measurable : It's crucial for goal achievement that you are able to track your progress towards your goal. That's why all goals need some form of objective measuring system so that you can stay on track and become motivated when you enjoy the sweet taste of quantifiable progress.

Achievable : Setting big goals is great, but setting unrealistic goals will just de-motivate you. A good goal is one that challenges, but is not so unrealistic that you have virtually no chance of accomplishing it.

Relevant : Before you even set goals, it's a good idea to sit down and define your core values and your life purpose because it's these tools which ultimately decide how and what goals you choose for your life. Goals, in and of themselves, do not provide any happiness. Goals that are in harmony with our life purpose do have the power to make us happy.

Timed : Without setting deadlines for your goals, you have no real compelling reason or motivation to start working on them.

By setting a deadline, your subconscious mind begins to work on that goal, night and day, to bring you closer to achievement.

Prioritizing Your Goals

Achieving challenging goals requires a lot of mental energy. Instead of spreading yourself thin by focusing on several goals at once, invest your mental focus on one goal, the most important goal right now. When you are prioritizing, choose a goal that will have the greatest impact on your life compared to how long it will take to achieve. A large part of goal setting is not just identifying what you want, but also identifying what you must give up in your life in order to get it. Most people are unwilling to make a conscious decision to give up the things in their life necessary to achieve their goals.

Visualization

Emotionalizing and visualizing your goal will help you create the desire to materialize it into your life. One of the best visualization tools is a vision board. Simply find a magazine, cut out pictures that resonate with the goal that you want to achieve, glue them onto a piece of poster board, and place that board somewhere that you can view it several times a day.
In order for visualization to work, it's necessary that you emotionalize your goal as much as possible. Create a list of the benefits you will see when you achieve your goal and concentrate on how that will make you feel.

Overcoming Procrastination

We all procrastinate from time to time. Procrastination occurs when we avoid tasks that we find unpleasant. Even if we perform other work-related tasks instead of the ones we dislike, we are guilty of procrastination. Unfortunately, procrastination will hinder our long-term success. With the proper skills, you can overcome procrastination.

Eat That Frog!

Mark Twain has a saying that applies to procrastination: If the first thing you do each morning is to eat a live frog, you can go through the day with the satisfaction of knowing that that is probably the worst thing that is going to happen to you all day long!

Brian Tracy named his course on time management "Eat that Frog" because of this saying. The frog is anything that you do not want to do. Basically, you should complete your dreaded tasks first. Getting them out of the way will provide you with a sense of accomplishment and keep you from procrastinating. Always begin with the task that is the hardest and most significant, and you will be less tempted to procrastinate on other activities.

Just Do It

When you dislike a particular task, it is easy to procrastinate. Whether you spend time checking email or looking at Instagram, you are procrastinating. You need to do more than identify when you procrastinate. You need to discover why.

• Discover your obstacles: What do you choose over your tasks?

• Discover ways to remove obstacles: Ask for support, and take action. For example, you could turn off the Internet and your phone.

• Reward yourself: Make the task fun, and use small rewards as incentive. Once you have identified your frogs and obstacles, the only answer is take action. Make the tasks that you want to avoid part of your daily routine. Schedule the tasks into your calendar. Once they become habit, you will find them easier to accomplish. Once you have scheduled the time to accomplish your tasks, you must follow through. Resist the temptation to procrastinate with your favorite time waster.

Just do it.

The 15 Minute Rule

Lack of time is a common excuse for not completing a task. We often overestimate the time that it takes to complete tasks, but the 15 minute rule allows you to accurately time your tasks. When you follow the 15 minute rule, you set a timer for 15 minutes and work on a task. You should stop working on the task when the time is up. You will be surprised by how many tasks you complete within the 15 minutes. When you are not able to complete a task within 15 minutes, schedule 15 minutes the next day for the same task. This allows you to make consistent progress. You will also be able to better estimate how long a similar task will take.

Chop It Up

The size of a project can also contribute to procrastination. It is easy to become overwhelmed by a large project. The key to overcoming procrastination is to chop up the large project into smaller tasks. Rather than looking at the entire project, focus on the single task. This will prevent you from becoming overwhelmed by the enormity of the work you must complete. For example, you could break a large report into different tasks such as brainstorming, outlining, writing, etc. This technique will create a sense of achievement with each step and improve motivation, allowing you to stay focused as you reach the end of the entire project.

Review Questions 1. What is the Frog? a) Boring task

b) Dreaded task

c) Important task

d) Unimportant task

2. The frog you begin with should be the hardest and _____.

a) Most complicated

b) Least complicated c) Most boring

d) Most significant

3. What is the action that you take when procrastinating?

d) Incentive

4. What will rewards provide? a) Obstacles

b) Identification of needs

5. What should you do if you have not completed the task within 15 minutes?

a) Cease the task

b) Continue working

c) Start over the next day

d) Time how much longer the task takes

6. What is a common excuse for not completing a task?

a) Disinterest

b) Not in job description c) Lack of time

d) Too complicated

7. What can happen when you are assigned large projects? a) Feel motivated

b) Feel overwhelmed

c) Avoid procrastination d) Planning is easy

8. What does completing small parts of a project create?

a) Feeling overwhelmed b) Motivation

d) Sense of achievement

9. What did Carl do when requesting information? a) Avoid conversation

b) Chat for 20 minutes c) Verify information d) Send emails

10. When did Carl finish the project? a) On time

b) A week late c) A day late d) Early

Just Do It

Consider the ways you procrastinate to answer the following questions.

What are your obstacles?

_____

_____

What steps can you take to overcome your obstacles?

How can you reward yourself for completing tasks? _____

_____
__ _____
_____ _____
_____ _____
_____ _____
_____ _____
_____
____ _____
_____ _____.

Chop It Up

Think of a task that you find overwhelming. In the space below, break it into smaller, more manageable tasks.

_____
_____
_____
_____
_____
_____
_____
_____

_____ _____
_____ _____
_____
__ _____
_____ _____
_____ _____.

Immediate goals

(Two weeks- One month)

1._____

 2._____

 3._____

___

Short term goals (One month-Three months)

1._____

 2._____

 3._____

___

Long term goals (Three months-One year)

1._____

_____ _____

_____ 2._____

_____ _____

_____

3._____

_____ _____

_____

People who fly into a rage always make a bad landing. Will Rogers

Anger Management Worksheet

CorporateTrainingMaterials.com Gaining Control

Anger is instinctual, yes. It is an emotion that comes unbidden and we often don't have a choice whether we would be angry or not.

What we can do however, is take control of our anger when it comes. In this module, we will discuss ways to gain control over our anger. Specifically we will discuss recognizing warning signs, coping thoughts, relaxation techniques and ways to blow off steam.

A Word of Warning

The first step in gaining control of anger is to recognize its warning signs. You have to be aware of symptoms that your anger is about to build up, so that you can catch yourself early and make the necessary intervention. This process involves taking yourself from the 'moment' and observing your own reactions from a third person point of view.

Warning signs of anger exists in a range. Some are very obvious; others very subtle. They differ from person to person.

Signs of anger can be physical, mental, emotional, and behavioral.

Emotional signs of anger include:

- sadness
- irritability • guilt
- resentment
- feeling like you need to hurt someone
- needing to be alone
- needing to isolate one's self
- numbness

Behavioral signs of anger include:

- clenching of fist
- pounding of fist on any surface
- pacing
- raising one's voice

- any act of aggression/ passive-aggression

Physical signs of anger include:

- rapid heart rate
- difficulty breathing
- headache
- stomachache
- sweating
- feeling hot in the face and neck
- shaking

Mental signs of anger include:

- difficulty concentrating
- obsessing on the situation
- thinking vengeful thoughts
- cynicism

Using Coping Thoughts

Once you realize that you are angry, or that you're about to get angry, you can start calming yourself mentally. The following are just a few mental scripts you can use to keep your anger under control.

- Calm down first, and think this through.
- This may not be as bad as it seems.

- This is just one incident --- it doesn't define my life.
- I am capable of managing this situation.
- It's alright to be upset. / I have the right to be upset in this situation. / I am angry.
- What needs to be done immediately? (Damage control/ solution-focused mode).
- Bad things/ Mistakes do happen/ Nothings says that things will go right all the time.
- There is no need to feel threatened here.
- I have no control over other people and their feelings. But I have control over myself.
- I have managed anger successfully before and I will again.

Using Relaxation Techniques

Another way to help you control your anger is to intentionally induce yourself to a state of calm. This can help especially in addressing the physical symptoms of anger.

Relaxation techniques that you can do include: 1. Breathing Exercises

Deliberately controlling your breathing can help a person calm down. Ways to do this include: breathing through one's nose and exhaling through one's mouth, breathing from one's diagram, and breathing rhythmically.

2. Meditation

Meditation is a way of exercising mental discipline. Most meditation techniques involve increasing self-awareness, monitoring thoughts, and focusing. Meditation techniques include prayer, the repetition of a mantra, and relaxing movement or postures.

3. Progressive Muscle Relaxation (PMR)

PMR is a technique of stress management that involves mentally inducing your muscles to tense and relax. PMR usually focuses on areas of the body where tension is commonly felt, such as the head, shoulders, and chest area. It's a way to exercise the power of the mind over the body.

4. Visualization

Visualization is the use of mental imagery to induce relaxation. Some visualization exercise involves picturing a place of serenity and comfort, such as a beach or a garden. Other visualization exercises involve imagining the release of anger in a metaphorical form. An example of this latter kind of visualization is imagining one's anger as a ball to be released to space.

5. Music

Some people find listening to music as very relaxing. The kind of music that's calming differs from person to person; traditional relaxation music includes classical pieces, acoustic sounds, and even ambient noises.

6. Art and Crafts

There are people who find working with their hands as a good way to relax. This is especially true for people who feel their tensions in their hands. Drawing pictures, paper construction and sculpting are just some of the ways to de-stress when faced with an anger trigger. Arts and crafts are helpful because it keeps a person from obsessing on the anger while he or she is still in the recovery phase of the anger cycle.

Blowing Off Some Steam

Another way of controlling your anger is by getting the anger energy out---blowing off steam. These techniques are especially helpful when you are in the crisis phase of the anger cycle.

The following are some constructive ways of blowing off steam:

1. Screaming

If the place would allow it, screaming can help release the tensions and frustrations that come with anger. Think of the thing that angers you the most, build momentum, and let it out in one big shout.

You may also scream out the words you wish you could say if the venue is appropriate; the louder the scream, the better.

2. Physical Activity

Many people find exercise, sports, dancing and even just pacing about, as effective ways to vent anger. This makes sense; if the fight and flight response gears a person for physical action, then physical action might indeed be the best way to deal with the anger. Physical activity is also believed to release endorphins, our natural mood regulators.

3. Pillow Punching

The need to fight back may be channeled through punching pillows. Pillows provide a safe way to release tensions; it's safe not just for the object of the anger but also for one's self. Related techniques include wringing out towels and breaking old plates.

4. Writing

If physical activities are not your thing, you can blow off

steam by expressing your thoughts and feelings in writing. You can write in an unstructured way, simply putting on paper the first thing that comes to your mind. You can also be more creative about it, and channel your anger through poetry or song.

5. Singing

Here's a new one: vent your anger by going to your nearest videoke or karaoke bar. Many people find singing therapeutic, especially if the song lyrics and melody matches one's mood. Stress Management Worksheet Corporatetrainingmaterials. com

Adopting the right attitude can convert a negative stress into a positive one.

Hans Selye Understanding Stress

To begin, let's look at what stress is. We'll also explore how stress can be positive and negative, and we'll look at the Triple A approach that will form the basis of this workshop.

What is Stress?

The Random House Dictionary defines stress as, "physical, mental, or emotional strain or tension," and, "a situation, occurrence, or factor causing this." The word "stress" actually comes from a Latin word meaning, "distress."

Stress can be difficult to pin down because it is a very individual thing. For me, public speaking is very stressful – but it may be one of your great joys in life. Remember this during this workshop: since stress is different for everyone, your approach must be

personalized, too. Typically, we interpret stress as a negative thing, but it doesn't have to be that way.

What is Eustress?

"Eustress" means stress with a positive effect. It was coined by psychologist Richard Lazarus in 1974.

How can stress be positive, you ask? Think of the emotional strain caused by these

positive events:

- Winning a race
- Being a new parent
- Riding a rollercoaster
- Watching a scary movie

In these situations, the physical, mental, or emotional strain actually produces positive emotions, rather than the negative emotions usually associated with stress. Without distress or eustress, life would be a pretty boring ride!

Understanding the Triple A Approach

In this workshop, we will give you three main ways to approach stress. It is important to remember that you have a choice! You can choose to:

- Alter the situation or your approach to it.
- Avoid the situation. • Accept the situation.

Before we explore this approach however, let's look at the foundation of a low-stress lifestyle.

Stress Management

Seeing the Humor

- Reading a funny story or joke can be a great way to make you laugh.
- Keeping a humorous calendar in your cubicle is a good way to have a laugh at hand particularly if it's the page-a-day type. Just make sure it's appropriate and permitted in your office.
- Seeing the humor in a stressful situation can be difficult, but it can also help you put things in perspective. Try to imagine how the situation might appear from the outside, or how you might see it down the road.

- Sharing a laugh with friends and family is always a good pick-me-up.

When sharing jokes at work, be sensitive to others, and make sure that what you're sharing is appropriate.

Deep Breathing

Deep breathing is an excellent relaxation tool that can be adapted for
almost any situation. It also has some
physical benefits, including:

- Reduction in blood pressure • Reduction in muscle tension • Boost in metabolism
- Clearing of the mind
- Boost in endorphins (our natural painkillers)

The basic technique is just like it sounds: slowly breathe in through your nose, and then breathe out through your mouth. Try counting slowly as you do this. Each breath should take ten to twenty seconds. (You will be able to take longer breaths with practice.)

When you are in a stressful situation, it is easy to unobtrusively deep breathe to keep yourself cool. This will also help prevent some of the harmful physical effects of stress, since stress causes us to breathe faster, making our bodies work harder.

If you have a few moments to yourself, sit down, close your eyes, and spend a few minutes deep breathing. Deep breathing can also be used in conjunction with picturing your sanctuary or stretching.

Creating a Stress Log

A stress log can help you identify your major stressors, and it can help you identify trends in those stressors. Identifying the cause of stress can help you reduce the number and impact stressors in your life, and it can help you manage the stress that does occur.

© Corporate Training Materials www.corporatetrainingmaterials.com

www.ingramcontent.com/pod-product-compliance
Lightning Source LLC
Chambersburg PA
CBHW070546300426
44113CB00011B/1802